CHICK

Hannah Lowe was born in Ilford to an English mother and Jamaican-Chinese father. She has lived in London, Brighton and Santa Cruz, California. She studied American Literature at the University of Sussex and has a Masters degree in Refugee Studies. She has worked as a teacher of literature and creative writing, and is now living in Newcastle studying for a PhD. Her pamphlet *The Hitcher* (The Rialto, 2011) was widely praised. Her first book-length collection *Chick* was published by Bloodaxe Books in 2013.

HANNAH LOWE

CHICK

BLOODAXE BOOKS

ISBN: 978 1 85224 960 1

First published 2013 by
Bloodaxe Books Ltd,
Highgreen,
Tarset,
Northumberland NE48 1RP.

www.bloodaxebooks.com
For further information about Bloodaxe titles
please visit our website or write to
the above address for a catalogue.

Supported by
**ARTS COUNCIL
ENGLAND**

Cover design: Neil Astley & Pamela Robertson-Pearce.

Printed in Great Britain by
Bell & Bain Limited, Glasgow, Scotland.

For my dad

ACKNOWLEDGEMENTS

A number of these poems first appeared in a pamphlet *The Hitcher* (The Rialto, 2011). My thanks to Mike Mackmin.

Some of these poems or versions of them have appeared in the following publications: *Ambit, Days of the Roses, The Delinquent, Iota, The Interpreter's House, Magma, New Writer Magazine, The North, Orbis, Out of Bounds* (Bloodaxe Books, 2012), *The Poetry Paper, Poetry Review, The Rialto, Sentinel Literary Journal, The Shuffle Anthology, The Spectator* and *Stand.*

The lines 'A gambler is never lonely. There's another man who wants his money' in 'Thunder Snakes' are adapted from Oswald 'Columbus' Deniston's contribution to *Windrush: The Rise of Multi-Racial Britain*, edited by M. Phillips & T. Phillips (Harper Collins, 1998).

I am very grateful to everyone who helped me along the way with this collection, in particular all those in the Advanced Poetry Workshop at The Poetry School.

My special thanks to John Glenday.

CONTENTS

Chick

We talked about you all the time.
Dan said he saw you ironing cellophane.
I said you'd let me hold a thousand pounds.
We found a hollow-soled shoe.

My cousins loved your tricks.
They'd follow the lady, search your sleeves,
blow luck into your fist. Mum called you a croupier.
At school I said you drove a cab.

Most days you were back at dawn.
I watched through a crack as you slept,
a hump of blankets in the purple light,
the smell of sweat.

I saw you once Dad, knelt over cards,
strewn on the floor, panic in your face.
For God's sake, Chick, you said.
You couldn't do the marks.

Then, each Tuesday, £16.30 – a paper,
tobacco, one hand of Kalooki. You sunk
into the settee like you'd been kicked there,
shouted in the bathroom, asked me for money.

At the wake, a ring of phlegmy men
with yellow eyes and meaty skin, told me
what your name meant, placed the ace of hearts
across your coffin, flowers shaped as dice.

Thunder Snakes

Darling, that gambling was in my blood,
was always there like thunder snakes
that slide in through an open door,
across the boards and coil under the bed.
The dice were my first friends, then lacquered tiles
of winds and dragons, plum, bamboo.

A gambler is never lonely. There's another man
who wants his money. He keeps the company
of kings and knaves, lies awake and flips them over
in his mind, while rain is spitting on the glass
and the anxious light of dawn
slides down the walls, across his body.

In Your Pockets

A roll of tens or twenties. *Tons*, you said
or *monkeys, plums*. I lifted what I could
for paint or felt-tip pens, you curled in bed
as I explored the shaded room, or stood
above you quietly, holding back my breath
to match the time of yours. After dinner,
you slapped cash onto the table-cloth
or fetched a fist of bracelets from the car,
a sack of dresses.
        It was easy, getting
what you wanted till you couldn't deal
a round of Pinochle or stop the trembling
of your hands around the steering wheel.
Then you were home. No need to snoop. All bets
were off. I didn't pick your empty pockets.

Five Ways to Load a Dice

Like the yellowed cubes of knucklebone
        they plucked from slag and ashes at Pompeii,
speared with pig bristle or flint
        to slow the roll.

Or like your father in the rattling alleys
        of Shanghai, who smelt his sweat among
the shooters crouched like toads around the felt,
        who breathed into his palms
to warm the wax he'd painted on. These ways are old.

Now juice joints play electric dice,
        magnetic woodlice curled inside, or tappers,
hollow chambers filled with mercury
        that slips from side to side.

In our house, dice the green of emeralds
        or ruby red like cola cubes
were hidden in a biscuit tin, behind the scarves
        and parkas in the cupboard in the hall.

There were rooms we didn't go in
        but I saw you once,
the door ajar, the curtains drawn against the sun.
        You were huddled like a scholar
in the lamplight – goggles and a dentist's drill,
        a pan of smoking lead, that smell.

Seven Card Stud

The dealer cuts and it begins, like known verses
or some sacred dance, each table of cads and plungers,
starved dunces, the cameras overhead, vents wired.

The House in black shirts and waistcoats
perch like ravens on high stools above the baize
or stand in basement caverns, eyes fixed to screens.

Close-ups of fanned cards, of men who look
like movie stars, men with scars and rutted skin,
scared men with naked faces.

The House crusade against crooks, card-counters,
sharks. In the dark church of cash-machines
spitting fifties, girls bring their lotions to the table,

trussed in gold dresses, hands rubbing under vests.
You can grip a lucky chip or wear red underpants,
your mother's crucifix, but talismans won't switch

a hand of duds or stop the rain outside at 6 a.m.
where your reflection whispers *cunt cunt cunt*
from the shining pavement, stunned.

My Father's Butterflies

Looked more like birds, I thought, made of paper,
tightly folded, edge to point to corner.
His fingers gently worked the lines and creases
so the wings would beat upon their axes
and the butterfly have life. I took
my bristle brush and ink and dabbed the look
I wanted on each one – ruby splashes,
careful petals, polka-dots, black dashes
on their backs – so they belonged to me.
In his palms, the painted paper body
rested like a pair of playing cards,
perhaps the ten of hearts and six of spades,
what faced me when he cut a deck in two
and told me: *blow on the butterfly!* And I blew.

Sharp

I have played at many tables

I have played with Manchester George
and Billy Falco

I have dealt hands
of Baccarat, Black Jack
and Chemin de Fer

I have laid a royal flush,
laid down nothing

I have heard the rasp
of a thumbed deck
as breathing

I have had the last pounds
of pilots, the last pounds
of housewives

I have played at many tables

I have blistered cards
with pins and scalpels

I have played with Tony Walker,
Black Alan and Paul from St Lucia

I have harboured a queen
in the curve of my palm

I have lost a thousand
on the horses

I have shaved the sides
of knaves and aces

I have wept in the car

I have played at many tables

Sausages

They hang from the washing line
between the tea towels and bleached sheets.
He has pegged them in neat clusters,
dark fingers of blood and gristle
with twisted ends and oily skins.
They flame against the trees.

She smells them from the backdoor –
ginger, clove and fennel. The house is quiet.
He is hiding from her. Her mother told her
*not to marry a foreigner. You always wanted
to be different* she hissed. *Now this. He's black
and old enough to be your father.*

The sausages are Chinese dragon red,
the red of a chilli, or a shamed face.
They gather fire, drying on her line.
This is Ilford, Essex, 1965.
The neighbours eat mince and cabbage
and talk about her.

She asked him not to do it
but they taste like home to him
and he is like good food to her.
Tonight they will eat sausages together
and she will lick the oil and spice
from his hands.

Self Portrait, Before Me

The smell of bonfires. Autumn in the garden.
My father holds my brother's tiny hand
beside the willow gone to sepia.
My brother's face is peering from his hood,
already looking from the centre, finding
other points of light. I'm years away.
This photo's edges lift before I'm born.
My father smiles his sudden smile, his eyes
are curled like fallen leaves. Behind, the pylons
stand above the tracks where trains run past,
the blur of scribbled figures in the glass
who cannot see our dying yellow garden
where the man and boy forever walk
the path towards my mother's camera.

The Other Family

(for Rob)

The boy blows bubbles
at the camera in a garden
of yellow roses,
then the woman blows them,
then the boy.
You tumble up
from a fake fall, your jaw
meeting the boy's fist,
his arms flailing wildly,
you unfurling punches
that don't connect,
don't come close to that,
dancing backwards on your toes
to the kitchen door.
This is years ago,
the woman at the sink
in an orange dress,
hands lost in the suds,
watching the man and boy spar,
the man teaching the boy
how to be a man, the boy
recalling a bubble's
holographic light, or upstairs,
the box room with its
wallpaper of bridges and blue trains
where he woke early to a spot
of sunlight on the skirting board
which made him think
of birds or god until he heard
your key click in the door.
And the woman downstairs
stacking dishes, thinking
of the night she woke in,
moonlight sliced across
the rug, the empty space

beside her, not knowing
where you were.
This is years ago.
The camera has stopped rolling
but we are spinning back,
frame by frame,
the boy, the woman,
you – driving in your car,
driving miles, all night,
with money in your pocket,
coming home
with what you know.

Dance Class

The best girls posed like poodles at a show
and Betty Finch, in lemon gauze and wrinkles,
swept her wooden cane along the rows
to lock our knees in place and turn our ankles.
I was a scandal in that class, big-footed
giant in lycra, joker in my tap shoes,
slapping on the off-beat while a hundred
tappers hit the wood. I missed the cues
each time. After, in the foyer, dad,
a black man, stood among the Essex mothers
clad in leopard skin. He'd shake his keys
and scan the bloom of dancers where I hid
and whispered to another ballerina
he's the cab my mother sends for me.

Anna's House

We pegged the sheets to make a hideaway
and huddled with your brothers, scanned the pages
of your father's shiny magazines,
a splay of naked teenagers. I think
the older brother knew much more than me
of what we did below the eiderdown
but if I cared at all, I don't remember.

I only see you Anna, sat cross-legged
on a pillow where the winter sun
had pooled its light and in the lemon glow
your glasses glittered. And the telly echoed
from the living room, your mother frozen
in its bluish glare, her hands like sparrows
crushed into her lap to stop their flutter.

And the younger brother was a cherub,
but victim of the slap and pinch, victim
in all kinds of ways I can't remember.
What I recall is lying in your bedroom
where the ceiling was a galaxy
of day-glo stars and planets, tiny moons,
the cluttered shelves of beads and china dolls

and you, a baby bird, so snappable,
the yellow hair that moulted where you sat
and how we never had a wink of sleep,
top-toeing in your single bed. At dawn,
you lay unmoving, ashen-faced, one hand
across your brow, your nightdress buttoned up
with little pearls. *We need to rest*, you said.

Strange Ann, at school I didn't talk to you
and only now it all comes back to me:
the wobbling beads of rain across the glass
and first light creeping slowly up the headboard
where you lay and wrung your hands and whispered
what I couldn't hear and turned away
to face the wall, and closed your tired eyes.

B-Boy Summer

It was the summer of the caterpillar.
Boys at the door in caps and shell-toe trainers
asking for my brother. Dan, re-branded,
baggy jeans and neon laces, cool kid
they should knock for now. Beautiful boys
in the flower garden rocked to the noise
of hip hop – Salt-n-Pepa, De La Soul.
I watched them, kneeling on the window sill,
Elijah spinning on a square of lino;
Richie waiting for the cue to throw
his body to the ground and applejack
or windmill; Charlie springing from his back
to land straight up, heroic, on two feet.
And later, at the bedroom door, the beat
of bass-line and their laughter as I waited
on the landing, little sister, loaded
with desire to be a boy, sixteen
and in the crew. On the gymnastics team
I was the best at backwards somersaults,
could fling myself one handed on the vault
but I was never a B-Girl, just a body
growing, loving boys who never saw me
in the silent garden where I'd go
alone to head-spin on the moonlit lino.

Jason

You showed me dead birds in the park.
We stayed out late, clambered over railings,

rang strangers' bells and ran. I didn't ask
about the rusty scabs, your bashed skin

until you were the runt of a new pack –
boys in West Ham shirts with slashed mouths,

bitten nails, their subways tagged in rage.
I craved you back, still played the tapes

you made me. I heard you put a brick
through somebody's front door.

You turned up one New Year's Eve,
three years older, moon-eyed, twitchy,

out of place. You punched a window –
a vane of glass punctured your hand.

I read what you did in the paper, *mindless, frenzied,*
a reporter phoned the house. I found a photo –

the only boy in the gymnastics team,
your goblin face squinting at the flash.

They found you in your cell. Too late
to unclench those fists as hard as stones.

Little rascal. You thud around my head
like a football kicked, and kicked again.

Barley Lane

Neeshat of the see-saw, I see your buckled shoes
	where teacher caught you in a photograph
and I am caped behind you, rising
	with black holes between my teeth

and Mina, flower-clips and tiny furry wrists I gripped
	to swing you on the grass
and Nirpal of my street who taught me hindi *ek do tin*
	and Lloyd McClean of number 53
who wore electric green, who smelt of coconuts,
	who smelt so good

and Helen Lawrence who I vowed to meet at midnight
	on the railway tracks, each night's betrayal
clicking neatly on the other
	like a tube of coloured polo sweets

and Katie Noon and Lucy Noon –
	your mother wept in Sainsbury's,
my mother said *not one, but two, not one, but two*
	and May who took front seat
and lived, a snake and ladder scar across her cheek.

And all the children of the pool
	bursting out of pastel cubicles
and all the children of the playing fields
	in pastorals with lunch packs under willow trees.

Joanna of the flute, Abida of the flute and Damon Edgar,
	first violin, waiting like a matron in the corridor
to hush us in to Christmas in the hall,
	a hundred wire-hanger mobiles strung with tinsel
turning in the air above us –
	Angels, Angels, I have lost you all.

Learning to Play

Brocade stool in the dark back room. Small hands cupped
around an orange. The smell of polish. Dropped
wrists raised by a pencil. Crotchet, minim, semi-breve.
Breath held for length of an eight note scale. The black feel
of the black keys. C Major, A Minor.
Conducting the air with a finger. A swarm of semi-quavers.
Rudiments of Music Theory: pianissimo, mezzo forte, adagio.
Adding the left hand. Legato, legatissimo.
The stern click of a metronome. Getting older, testy.
The calm of a treble clef's fat body,
thin tail. Tonic triads. Two hand chromatics.
Hours in the window on baroque minuets. Minutes
in the exam room. Another woman's piano.
The beat of your own time, poco a poco.
Triplets, trills, the bite of a mordent. More practice. Rages.
Your grandfather's music, curled yellow pages.
The smell of discipline. His signature scratched
like a tightly pulled bootlace. Notes squashed
like flies on the stave. Muzio Clementi, Debussy, Satie.
Umbrellas in the rain. Dolente, dolore.
Rachmaninov. Saved for these adult hands, *Allegro Animato*.
Eyes shut: G flat Major, four octaves, staccato.

Room

I miss that room we shared for a year,
off the boardwalk, downtown Santa Cruz, both smitten
with the landlord, an East Coast skate-boarder

who wore a beanie hat and used our names often
and with meaning. Behind his bedroom door
a blue light glowed on pots of cannabis – *my children*,

he said. This was how we found the spiders,
scuttling on the walls and through our sheets.
We found them in our clothes and shoes, our hair.

We returned to that room from days at the beach
where cold Pacific waves had pulled us under,
shocked us from the searing heat,

the fog of drugs and drink, enough to start over
at sundown. One evening, at the Lotus Laundromat
I met a boy who bought me dinner

on the freeway: nachos, pinto beans with pork fat,
enchiladas, sour cream. We went dancing
in a clammy room behind the Silver Bullet,

slamming shots that blurred the bar, bent double laughing
at the pallid cowboys sat alone, their slimy ponytails
and pock-marked skin, their chequered bellies spilling

over jeans. I turned twenty-one next day and dialled
my mother from a greasy booth along the Boulevard,
sobbed soundlessly into the static fuzz as punk-haired girls

flew by on roller skates, a tramp with tattooed stars
under his eyes was thumping on the glass. An orange Dodge
pulled up and I climbed wordlessly into the car

beside a man I'd seen the week before. We rode
down Soquel Avenue, past clapboard coffee bars
and carousels rotating under pink and violet strobes,

hippies lolling on the sidewalk with their wrecked guitars.
There is something fine about the dawn walk home
from a strangers' house, the blue shore

hazed against the sky, the sun's defiant beams
and boys already rattling down the asphalt drives,
bent low on coloured boards, their arms
flung wide as though about to fly.

Fist

When my brother put his fist through a window
on New Year's Eve, no one noticed until a cold draft
cooled our bodies dancing. There was rainbow light
from a disco ball, silver tinsel round the pictures.
My brother held his arm out to us, palm
upturned, a foot high spray of blood.
This was Ilford, Essex, 1993, nearly midnight,
us all smashed on booze and Ecstasy and Danny,
6 foot 5, folding at the knee, a shiny fin of glass
wedged in his wrist. We walked him to the kitchen,
the good arm slung on someone's neck,
Gary shouting *Danny*, Darren phoning
for an ambulance, the blood was everywhere. I pressed
a towel across the wound, around the glass
and led him by the hand into the garden, he stumbled
down into the snow, slurring *leave it out* and *I'm OK*.
A girl was crying in the doorway, the music carried on,
the bass line thumping as we stood around my brother,
Gary talking gently saying *easy fella*, Darren
draining Stella in one hand and in the other, holding up
my brother's arm, wet and red, the veins stood out
like branches. I thought that he was dying,
out there in the snow and I got down, I knelt there
on the ice and held my brother, who I never touched
and never told I loved, and even then I couldn't say it
so I listened to the incantation *easy fella*
and my brother's breathing,
felt him rolling forward, all that weight, Darren
throwing down his can and yelling *Danny, don't you dare*
and shaking him. My brother's face was grey,
his lips were loose and pale and I
was praying. Somewhere in the street,
there was a siren, there was a girl inside
who blamed herself, there were men with blankets
and a tourniquet, they stopped my brother bleeding,
as the New Year turned, they saved him,
snow was falling hard, they saved us all.

Fathers Are Dancing with Their Sons

Fathers are dancing with their sons
in cities all across America.
In cowboy boots and tattered Stetsons

they enfold their boys and saunter
into spins and do-si-does and reels,
steps they knew in high school now remembered,

how they swayed with barefoot girls –
scent of bluebells, swirl of cotton dresses.
Now they clasp their sons in sluggish twirls,

boys who lay their heads against their fathers' chests,
their own hearts ripe with girls who cartwheel
in the shadows of the apple trees

or hard and heavy with the memories
of gentle hands. They loop their arms around
their fathers, who too have closed their eyes to see

the faces of their wives, or loamy ground
of cattle, fields of barley, hemp and maize
before the earth was drowned

by rain and black fruit fell and stained
the green floor of America. Now they softly steer
their sons through dancehalls in New York, Des Moines,

Los Angeles, to dance in coloured light of chandeliers,
the music from the carousel, their numbers
chalked by men with canes and velvet blazers.

Watch them turning slowly through the hours
or see them huddled in the box-cars,
riding through the night to sunrise over
any city in America.

Foxes

My friend complains about the foxes screaming
in his garden. Says he's menaced by the sound
and sees their snarling faces. I dress and go around
to help him. We listen to the night. His fingers
trace across my scars and smooth the skin
between until I catch his hand under my hand.
My newest bra is hanging on the headboard,
makes a shadow-rabbit on his ceiling.
We mix our noises with the foxes until dawn
when he takes my arm and coaxes me from bed
and down to the back-steps. I've been led
out here before. The ivy spills over the walls
in black and green, the sun makes streaks of red
across the sky. The foxes must be sleeping, sated.

Artisan du Chocolat, Borough Market

So I unwind my body from yours and I clamber from bed
to cross over the river and find myself here
in this little patisserie just off the market,

its countertop loaded with bright yellow cupcakes
and chocolate eggs wrapped in ribbon and tissue.
I order hot chocolate, so thick it stands up,

while in between mouthfuls, the girl to the right of me
talks of her therapist, whether she'll move to the suburbs
or stay in the city. *I'm lonely* she says to her friend

who is nodding, her mouth full of tart that is topped
with glazed apple. The waiter is yawning, leant on the counter,
chocolate smears at the sides of his mouth.

Through the window I see that the stalls have packed up
and the sky now is gathering and darkening as though it might sigh.
You are leaving tomorrow and here we all are

with the gateaux and pastries, the windows steamed up
and our hands round our mugs as we lull
our poor hearts with sweetness and sugar.

Now That You Live in Hoxton

All summer I talked about moving to Hoxton
or Shoreditch as though it was Streatham
that caused all our fights. We were bored, I said,
done with the chicken emporiums, pound shops
and chain pubs, no matter we'd fallen in love
in *The Crown* over pre-packed lasagne and 2-4-1 pints.
I saw us in Spitalfields market on Sundays,
the pheasants and quails bound with twine overhead,
the stalls selling chutney in old fashioned jars,
the coffee shops full of ethereal girls wearing
polka-dot shoes who you watched as I browsed
through the second hand volumes of poetry,
reading you lines out aloud, and we'd round off the day
at a bar in a long-ago factory, trussed
in impossible jeans we could barely sit down in
and flat caps we'd bought from a peeling boutique
where the shopkeeper told us we looked like
an advert for happiness.

Ink

Tor's off to *The Night of the Senses* annual ball to collect her award.
We buy a sailor's hat, a corset, seamed white fishnets
from a market stall in Elephant.

I read Columbians write messages of love on money –
Gordis, my love has no price, Memo. The central bank
has launched a TV campaign to wean them off the habit.

Seems that everyone at lunch is pregnant again. I paint
my life in lurid detail. Let them sip lemonade
and see what they're missing.

Siobhan talks about taking off. At *Brechon Bouton*, it's Paris.
In *El Rincon*, it's Peru or Chile. I know what I'm brave enough for
and it's not that, but I can eat steak so rare it's blue.

In Iran, tampering with bank notes is a crime. Students wrote
'Death to Dictator' on hundred rial notes, defaced
the Shah with spectacles and moles

which reminds me of Lenny, driving his cab in LA.
He left Tehran in a car boot, hasn't seen his family in fifteen years.
Chicago gave him asthma but Venice Beach was A-OK.

I write his story in my notebook, which these days
is what I do. A photo arrives in the post of my dad
on a roof in Notting Hill. He's holding a baby

who isn't me. At sixteen he left Jamaica, played poker
for his passage, worked the beetroot farms in Texas,
passed through Canning Town, E16. Some people never stop moving.

Tor gets in at 6. I've been up all night too. There's a tattoo
on her shoulder, cupid pulling on his bow. On her bicep,
a dollar sign. I lick my thumb and rub it. She laughs when it smudges.

Early Morning Swim

I'm too early to swim so I kill time wandering
through Brixton, the moon still out
over Atlantic Road, Electric Avenue.
It's quiet, perhaps it's dangerous for a girl
to be walking at 6.30 a.m. but I know these streets
and in the strange December warmth, I raise
my hand to the halal men in their bloody robes,
already busy with their knives and bones
and bright chunks of meat. I should be in the water
but instead, I pass the shuttered shops and slats
usually stacked high with yam and bananas,
the red awnings of the Wing Tai Market
where you can buy five types of black bean
and watch a beautiful boy sluice fish guts
into plastic buckets. There's a woman
stacking bread in the window of Greggs,
one in headphones sweeping the arcade,
another darts across my path on twitchy legs,
midriff exposed. She turns for a second
and meets my eye. I pass by The Havana Social
where a decade ago I danced all night
under wooden beams and drank bright pink
strawberry Daiquiris and shots of Sambuca.
Now plyboard seals the door and windows,
the name peeled to flecks of white. Daylight rises
on Electric Lane. By noon, the bearded man
in black tunic and knitted cap
will be frying lamb and onions in his van,
the Tunisians crowed at the pavement tables,
drinking coffee, rolling cigarettes. I should be
swimming but instead I'm watching the huge
Dragon Stout truck reverse down an alley,
its tarpaulin daubed in orange flames.
It leaves me where I'm standing at 7.03 a.m.
by the red brick of Brixton Rec. They've got
a thousand tons of water waiting in there,
up the stairs, through the rotating doors,
below the new neon sign.

What I Think About When I'm Swimming

Legs.
>The thick, muscular legs of men
>>I do not know.
>The water is my friend. It holds us all.
Is it beautiful
>to watch me swim? Like the paddlewheel
>>of an old steam boat I go.
The time I couldn't swim, sunlight blanking out
>the children's faces where I surfaced,
flailing in a riot of rubber rings and screams.
>Now I cannot drown,
>>I keep the steady course,
I only hear the water babble in my ear,
>the fizz of bubbles from the man in front
who sprints with the ego of a fish,
>>new to these parts.
>It is boring to watch me swim.
What is beautiful are the tiles
>with their century of rust,
>>the pool spread like a sunken ballroom,
marbled with the winter sun and here,
>the deep end's edge
where I hang breathless,
>wet and warm and sad
>>and the warehouse roofs rise up
beyond the glass,
>like a painting of another land.

The Water Holds It All

Morning, and the bronzed god cracks the water's turquoise pane,
    sprints the fast lane for an hour in lime-green trunks
and underwater mp3. *It's Your Body, You Can Do It*
    tongues a satin voice into his ear.

The tattooed boy who never swims, stakes his corner
    when the amputees come hopping to the edge.
Their knee stumps spin away from him. The anorexic lady
    swishes on her back and dreams of vanishing, the pale fat man

sails gravely on. Music echoes in the rafters during lunch
    as Eva box-steps by her tape recorder,
high above the ladies in the water, sluggish ballerinas
    wading grapevines, mambo cha cha and after,

all the cool kids slip into the pool – Latino girls
    in cherry-print bikinis, ribs like xylophones.
Their skin's soft down is glinting where they dip and bob
    and ripples hula at their hips. The bull-necked boys

in thick gold chains and baggy shorts are flexing
    for the cock-a-doodle hurtle to the end and back, all splash
and muscle, jutting pectorals. The girls laugh into each other's shoulders.
    Everybody's coming out for coke and enchiladas.

At night, the pool is a sad cathedral. The broken-hearted
    float the shallows in fluorescent light or tug their goggles off
to weep, or slump over the side, tracing names into the blue.
    The penitents and self-beraters clock their miles

or skull along the floor with bloated cheeks and flowering hair.
    The moon does what it dares to on the water's surface.
The guard keeps death-watch from his pedestal then locks the door
    and dims the light. The water takes a breath and seals itself again.

Antonio, in the Coffee Shop

My love, I find you in the coffee shop
on Worship Street, two Sundays since we met,
since you winked and told me to come back.

The poets, if we call them that, are sat
or slumped in chairs. I'm at the side among
the bread and cakes: Amalfi lemon tart,

a *Torta Claudia*, an almond flan
someone's baked with love. The room is humming
with the smell of sage and parmesan.

You bring me coffee and a wedding ring
I hadn't seen before is tightly sunk
into your finger's flesh, a woman turning

from the shadows of the kitchen sink
to spread a smile and lick her fingertips
at you. Oh Antonio, you wink

at her! How many times you must have wiped
an errant splotch of cream or buttermilk
or icing from that perfect chin, those lips?

Now one by one, the poets stand to speak
their litanies of love, regret and grief.
There is a roll of fat between your neck

and scalp. There is a mole, a greasy raisin
on her shoulder blade, which you forgive,
which you have gently tantalised between
your teeth, Antonio, which you must love.

Yogapoint, Brixton

Vedavit, cross-legged in white cotton,
       hands cupped and idle in his lap,

waiting
       in a pale hall with skylights,

steel door propped open
       on an alleyway

of cracked stone,
       dead grass.

Vedavit,
       of soiled rooms

in Harpuhey, Mosside
       and other bleak addresses he forgets,

nearly forty, dragging mats
       and orange bolsters on the shiny floor,

strong animal,
       broad-backed,

slabs of muscle in his thighs.
       What if no one comes?

Vedavit, reborn and supple,
       with certificates,

the peace of understanding on his face,
       stood in the slant sun,

hands pressed in a fin
       that guides him.

On his knuckles,
        fading letters, sad blue Hate Love.

What if no one comes
        to stretch against his shoulders

or lie surrendered,
        calves scooped into his palms

or sit cross-legged
        sukhasana

breathing   breathing
        in the light of Vedavit's benevolence,
           his blessing?

Frank, at the Canal

And that fella went to give me 20p
for hours, hours, fixing his bike.
I worked my *socks* off there
and look at my hands will you,
20p and look at my hands

      I said don't worry. I'd rather, rather

You're a good person, Hannah.
Pixie Blue loves you.
He's a baby, aren't you? He's not a dog, he's just a baby

I'm happy, Hannah. I sleep down the way,
I've got my hammock,
we get so cosy, me and Pixie Blue,
we'd rather stay in bed all day

Sometimes I stand dead still,
      look up at the buildings
and the ground starts swaying,
      god it spins   I get so dizzy there, do you?

But I'm good at looking down, I can
      look down all right
from my hammock, me and Pixie Blue
      fifteen feet above it all

See that swan? His name is Caesar.
He knows me
      and I know him
They fixed his wing with wire, oh it's *cruel* I know
but what else could they do?

Some fucker tried to hook him
round the throat – what sort of person – that bastard
broke his wing, they had to fix him.
Oh it's cruel

I like Rhianna, yep she's good, she's good,
she makes me laugh. I like
John Betjeman – you see his statue there
inside Kings Cross?

I was in the RAF, I was   Oh god, I'm fucked, I'm full of booze

       I came from Belfast, thirty years ago

They killed my mother so they did.
My nephew robbed her, beat her, for, you guessed it,
crack cocaine

Come up on my lap, good boy, you Pixie Blue you

He's only eighteen months, a pup, he likes
a bit of cider, not too much

Johnny

Before there was a man on the pavement,
there was a man falling. There were
nineteen floors of glass and concrete
and a baby in the penthouse
screaming. Two girls in green kimonos
waited in a doorway, nineteen floors
above the street, watching
as he climbed across their balcony,
one foot on theirs, one foot on his,
saying *careful Johnny*, sweeping back their hair,
his knuckles blanching on the railings,
face contorted with resolve, knowing
there was no other way but this, this risk,
his trousers taut then tearing
as he slipped and fell. And even
as the fall began he only saw
the saucepan on the hotplate boiling,
the knife he'd used to chop
the carrots lying lethal on the board,
the baby who was nearly walking,
stretching up her hand towards
the handle of the pan, the handle
of the knife. Oh, he was tumbling
from the baby, his flat door
clicked and locked behind him, the girl
in her kimono standing on the doormat
saying *Johnny, there's a mouse,*
her perfume curling his nostrils, cartoons
playing in the background
where the baby in her bouncer
laughed, was really laughing
at the clumsy purple cat, the clever
budgie dancing in its cage, oh
how could there be a mouse
on the nineteenth floor, how could
his keys be on the wrong side
of the door, how could he cartwheel
through the air past all this glass and stone,
how would the baby ever understand.

Jack's Milk

Jack in the morning, glugging pints of milk
or naked on the bedroom floor
or flexing muscle armour in the mirror,
head bulky as a cow's, a red-haired hulk.

Afternoons, he scams the high street punters,
black sacks of watches in his fists, or stalks the Common,
cooing, ripping crusts for ducks and swans.
Or later in *The Rat and Carrot* find him cornered,

swinging punches under Christmas lights, sad ogre
galumphing through the night; nuzzles like a baby
under blankets, dreams himself a baby
waddling on the curb in filthy diapers,

giant freckled baby wailing in the kitchen,
Mum slurring lullabies or weeping
at the table, Mum at the counter swaying,
forking corned beef from a can.

Letter to William

William, my cousin, little Will.
I took the blame for the hand you sliced
ice-skating on the old back door
laid flat on the frosted grass. Now
you stalk the hill where Nine Ladies
were turned to stone, shield the circle,
hang your banners in the trees.
Soldier of a ragged clan
with your knife-sheared scalp and piercings
and a three-legged dog called Sweep.
He guards you as you shiver-sleep
at the quarry's edge and your breath
rips out in streaks of white. He woke
the camp from dawn's narcotic fog,
a tent ablaze. You raced through flames
of kerosene, too late too late,
those girls already burnt and gone.
Carpenter, you only come home
Christmastime, look too much older,
rib-thin, eyes like splinters. Still
you work the smooth curve of a lute
with sandpaper and plane, sing
I Loved a Lass and *Barb'ry Allen*,
claw your crooked face like something's
burrowed there. Thirteen years
you've been away, with your homebrew
and tobacco tin. They say
you're going blind. See you next time,
where I dream you, at the coast Will,
dog and girl, warm caravan.
Safe. The sky as big as any.

Reggae Story

My father liked the blues and Lady Day.
He left Jamaica way before the reggae
rocked all night in backstreet studios,
before King Tubby or Augustus Pablo.
But I used to love a boy who loved
dub reggae, loved thick lugs of ganga, loved
on Sunday nights to cross the river, take me
to The House of Roots and Aba-shanti
in the cobbled arches under Vauxhall
where the Lion of Judah decked the walls
and stacks of speakers pumped electric bass,
a single bulb above the smoky haze
and on the stage a little dreadlocked man
like Rumpelstiltskin shouted *Jah!* and spun
his blistering tunes on a single turntable
and shut-eyed men called back over the vinyl
Jah Rastafari. Next door, the old guys
were like wizened goats with yellow eyes
hunched over games of chess and ginger tea,
below the golden framed Haile Selassie,
king of kings. That boy didn't know my father
was a white-haired godless pensioner
and reggae music never really got me
until I played it on my own: Bob Marley,
U-Roy, Johnny Clark, and even then
it came like hymns or Faure's *Requiem*,
Vivaldi's *Gloria.* That boy thought I had
a Rasta like Prince Far-I for a dad
not the silent island man who sat
beyond the bedroom door I'd listen at
to catch a woman croon a melody:
I can't give you anything but love, baby.

Three Treasures

Jamaica in the attic in a dark blue trunk,
sea-salt in the hinges. What must it look like
all that wide blue sea?

England downstairs in a rocking chair.
Nanna rocking with her playing cards,
cigs and toffee, tepid tea

Jamaica frying chicken in the kitchen,
pig-snout in the stewpot,
breakfast pan of salt-fish, akee

China in the won-ton skin,
gold songbird on the brittle porcelain,
pink pagoda silk settee

Jamaica in the statues, lignum vitae heads
of dreadlocks. Anansi, rebel spider
in the storybooks, the poetry

England eating peaches on the patio,
hopscotching, Mum in wellies, secateurs
around the rosebush and the raspberries

England painting midnight with a sparkler,
cousins throwing Guy Fawkes on the bonfire,
orange ash confetti

England for the English in graffiti
on the roundabouts and bus shelters,
Please Sir! on TV

Jamaica on the phone at 3 a.m.,
my father's back-home voice through fuzz
and crack: *My friend, long time no see*

China in the Cantonese he knew
but wouldn't speak, in letters stuffed
in shoe-boxes, ink-stick calligraphy

China in his slender bones,
in coral birds of stitched bamboo,
China in an origami butterfly, that flew

Poem with a Plantain in It

(after Robert Hass)

Plantains are of course related to bananas
the colour of which
has often reminded me of custard.
How good it is that we slice
bananas into hot custard
and call this dessert. I must not
be led away from plantains.

I remember how the first plantain
appeared in our cupboard.
It was a week since you had premiered
the avocado, a year already since
the lychee. There was a boy at school
who had never seen a pepper
and this, you said, was a true sadness.

I must stay with plantains but it is worth
mentioning that there are three hundred and fifty
types of banana of which only one is exported
by the United Fruit Company.
There are pygmy bananas and red bananas
and bananas called lady fingers
but there are no bananas as big as a plantain.

The Caribbean café on the hill serves fried plantain
for breakfast. I am slightly in love with the waiter
who looks like the sculpted head
we bought back from Jamaica with his fine bones
and corn-rowed hair. The coffee he brews
is so strong my heart skips a beat.
This is not a metaphor.

Unpeeled, those bright supermarket bananas
have pale and yielding throats,
so different from the plantains
I buy in Brixton market
with their mucky skins
that snag like stuck zips,
their tough and pungent flesh.

Love

Mornings, we'd find salmon bagels from Brick Lane,
char siu buns and Soho flower rolls,
a box of Motichoor.

Upstairs, you huddled in the covers, curtains drawn,
the talk show murmur from the radio,
a stave of light across the wall.

New Flour, with Old

I

Lorna writes from Canada: *The year was 1970.*
Your daddy drove me down to Brixton & we parked up
on a side street strung with winter mist.

Watch, he said, watch this. A woman in a house dress
and wooden slippers hung at a shop door
calling out for half pound a salt fish and big gill a oil.

She was a ghost from my past, backwater Jamaica.
Men sat on the low wall and everyone so poor,
just making out, just enough.

What's changed from home, he said. Shopkeeper bedding rocks
of salt in mackerel to weight it down, puffing new flour with old.
A man like my father, your daddy said.

II

I lie in my room on the hill watching *Babylon* again.
Brixton, 1980, flickers blue on the screen.
I always want The Ital Lions to win,

who doesn't? I like the Indian mogul with his singsong accent
selling exclusive Kingston vinyl on Cold Harbour Lane.
Brixton is a bombed out maze

where police hunt early hours black boys.
What's changed is that today is March 10th 2012
and the sun comes out for the first time in months.

III

Gentrification doesn't shift the corner prophets
but doubles them. A new man in neon yellow cross
gestures wildly on a crate

and outside Boots a bible sound clash makes us laugh,
so great is the stake in our salvation. I buy
a handmade cupcake in a papier-mâché box

and fair-trade flat white from The Coffee Federation
but someone's son still got chased last week
from Blacker Dread to Loughborough Junction

and died by a wall on Moorlands Estate,
five bicycles racing away as we ate Honest Burgers,
licked our fingers in the market, sweet dim sum.

Siobhan says I'm part of it, but I say this is just a place I live.
The American bookseller and I wax on
about how change must be a good thing.

Rosa, his dog, has a new green blanket
beside Plays and Poetry. She's still queen of the sofa,
knows what she likes, and where she belongs.

Grandmother

My grandmother comes calling
on cold nights in England.
She is no old lady.

She wears honey-coloured stockings,
red dresses
with nipped waists,

paints her nails exotic flower shades,
smells of oranges,
hibiscus.

Lord girl, she says, from the end of my bed
How come you white?
How come so tall?

And she mutters Cantonese to my bedroom walls.
And when I wake
she's at the mirror,

scratching in her eyebrows
with a charred end
of a match,

saying *Mister Walwyn Pennyfeather.*
I curse the day I heard
that name.

1918

(after Ha Van Vuong 'Boy with Bamboo')

I saw you on the gangplank Grandfather,
stood in the fevered sun with your chin raised up.

Nothing in this strange new world could faze you,
not the grave black faces on the dock,

the bone-thin men, the women in stained dresses;
not the rash-faced guards who read your papers,

their orders unfurling on pointed fingers, fingers
that gripped your wrists, and split open your mouth

to count your teeth. I saw you there, heaving
through the crush, searching out the voices

from the hold, small men with bright black hair,
sea-eyes like yours. And if I saw you there,

didn't I see you on the other side,
stepping through the silver daze of rain

on the Shanghai wharf with no one behind you
waving goodbye, and nothing to go back to?

Didn't I see you, where the mountains puncture
the sky and the plains are cold and blue,

a river slicing through the troubled earth
where rusted shacks squat low. Didn't I see you,

peering through the reeds, small barefoot boy,
crouched down, with an armful of bamboo?

House Painting

The first time that you died was a rehearsal.
The ladder, propped among the climbing roses,
slid from under you and jammed the door-bell
in a shrill and constant toll that brought us
from our Sunday tasks. You lay stone-still
across the path with palms serene in prayer
above your chest, a strew of bloody petals,
mother asking *why's he lying there?*
again, again.
               We never knew who called
the ambulance. The neighbours came, a flock
of mourners. Cuban George, who smelt of ale
and something sour, led me off and locked
his arms around me, swaying. *Don't fear, don't fear*
about your daddy he murmured in my ear.

Homescape

My father laughing at the bathroom mirror,
orange razor in his hand,
three nicks on his chin stuck with tissue.
Why can't I see this clean?

Instead, blood seeps onto a T-shirt
balled in the drawers of my brother's room,
dries as a crust at the side of his mouth
and my own blood splashes on the wall again.

My father, dead these twelve years,
and in half the photographs I have,
his small hands raise up babies to the camera,
half hide his own shy smile,

the same smile I remember the Saturday
he rang the bell, waiting on the doorstep,
one eye sealed shut, unshaven,
wanting to come in.

Hospital Night

That crescent moon of flesh they've cut away
has got you singing morphine-serenades
to all the pretty nurses on the ward.
Forty years unwind to speakers playing

old calypso from a battered car;
a taxi slices light across the yard
on Orange Avenue and there you are,
dancing for your life.

Smoke

You are shouting down the corridor,
Han? One cigarette? If I turn back
I'll see you in your dressing gown,
slippers flapping at your heels,
your hair a wilful nest of grey.
I'll see you wheel your drip,
rubber tubing plugged
into your hands and chest.
So I walk on, past prints of trees
and silver birds, because I've seen you
on your knees Dad, searching
through the kitchen bin
for last night's puckered butts,
three deep stale drags,
these last few years, always
out of luck and on the blag.
If I turn back, I'll see your body,
split and stitched but still the crow
that's picking through your guts
is fattening up. And though
I've told you no three times,
still you're shouting *Han?*
So I go on, through plastic doors,
upstairs, across the foyer, let
the night air swoop across my face.

Fishes

The doorbell rings all week while you are lying
      in the single bed downstairs, the curtains holding back
the winter light. Someone laughs in the kitchen.
      Everybody's smoking. *Your daddy dying, girl.* Barbara
with her Tupperware of rice and peas. Last week
      you called for this. Now we trickle water on your lips
and like a child, you lick, some instinct deep within you
      craves this small relief. Tuesday, Auntie Dy
is on the doorstep, saying *Hello Han* as though a decade
      hasn't passed and suddenly I'm in her arms, my aunt
who disappeared, returned. The doctor, shiny headed, African,
      calls you Mr Lowe, shouts *Please Sir, can you hear me?*
We speak in whispers at the door. He tell us what the night
      will bring. I see your brain cells then,
a thousand small fishes, crossing the ocean.

Manchester George

(for Jock)

We used to drive for hours, Chick and me. Games in Canning Town and Forest Gate, or up the M1 – someone's uncle's pub, someone's front room. This was 1965. I drank in The Cubana, five nights out of seven, down from Manchester, missing my pals, liking a girl who didn't look in my direction. One night she'd gone and I drank on my own until just as I had my hat on, someone stepped through the wall – that's what it looked like. But it was panelled door and the whole wall folded away and there it was – spotlights and bright baize tables, a little casino – I couldn't believe it. Forty of them sat and stood, Chick in the middle dealing Chemmy, dealing Baccarat. He had on a good suit, like he was dressed for an occasion. And he shuffled the desk so fast and swish, like pulling ribbon through his hands, a real showman. That was the night I met him.

People knew him. We walked into rooms and people knew him. One night at The Victoria the boss came down and said *Not tonight Chick*, please, the three of us at the door, because the game was rigged – they didn't want him in because he'd win and they knew it. *Not tonight, Chick?* like it was a favour. After, your dad laughing in the rain. We drove down to The Old Friends in Whitechapel and ate Chinese ribs – first time I'd had Chinese. Your dad loved to boast, he said *George, I can make these better.*

He didn't save money because he always got it. It didn't matter. Honestly, he always had it.

I had so much respect for him, because he was older. Because he'd come all the way from Jamaica, from America, and he spoke about politics and religion and he was clever. He drove me everywhere, always talking, saying *George, did you ever think about it this way?* We sat all night at the kitchen table, light coming up the walls at 5 a.m., the ashtray full. Chick talking, dealing, his hands vanishing the deuce of spades, the three of diamonds, gone behind his tie, up his sleeve. I couldn't get it. He said *George, just look* and slowed it right down, and I felt like a boy again, like I wanted to please him. So that was how I learnt.

No, I won't come in if he's asleep. You know I went to see him the first time at St Luke's. He was so thin. He said *George, they've taken half my stomach* but he still sat up and sang to the nurses. I'd best be off but do you know I was with him the night you were born? We got back to your mum's at dawn and wet your head. He never drank. I drank, but your dad, never. So the only thing you had was Cinzano. The two of us like a pair of girls. It was a heat-wave that summer. All the ladybirds were dying. No rain in three months but that night it came down, when you were born.

You know I've got this place in Spain now? I did all right. After, you and your mum come over. I'll bring you the keys. I'll get your flights. I did all right. We made a lot of money.

Is he very bad? I won't come in. But when he wakes up, tell him George came by? George, from Manchester.

Six Days in March

At the end of his life, my father slumped
in his chair, the old mustard cardigan
unbuttoned, his hair gone wild, cartoonish.

A dismembered chicken rested on the table,
mashed swede, mashed potato.
He watched me eat,

his own plate pushed aside,
my cousins tucking in, the dog at my feet
begging. Intermittently, he raised his knife

letting out a sigh we all ignored
until finally he said my name.
He said *you know I'm going to die*

and I said *Dad, not now*
and he said *can you stay a while?*
and I said nothing.

*

No dignity in this.
We find you on the stairs,
old child in tears. You want to piss

      and so I carry you,
the weightless body folded in my arms.
      The house is smaller, brighter.

I pass the doorway quickly
      where my mother holds your face,
a bowl of milky water on her knee, a razor.

The nurses come, their blue efficiency,
their muscled hands. They twist you on the sheets
      and lay you naked, powdered, clean.

The shocking body in the light,
        bone and paper skin,
the ladder on your shins of buckle scars,

        thighs so slight and girlish,
your penis dumb and nuzzled
        in its bed of hair.

*

So this is what I'm left with.
A stained brown cufflink box lined
with stained red silk,

two black elastic loops, one snapped and frayed.
        I hold it to my nose, search out
the sweat-and-tobacco smell of his hair, his clothes,

the old yellow cardigan. What's a life made of?
        Fifteen pounds in a post office account,
a notebook scrawled in horses' form,

one photograph of three Jamaican aunts
        in white lace dresses, straight-backed
with clasped hands under a palm tree?

Say

Say that your mother took in a lodger.
An old man say, down on his luck,
mostly out of the house
or asleep, no bother.

Say they grew closer, his voice in the kitchen,
her laughter, his old-fashioned shoes
next to yours in the hall.
Say he sometimes cooked dinner –

the four of you eating lasagne.
Your mother was plumper and happier.
Say you were eating your pudding
(hot custard, banana)

and all of a sudden the lodger was standing
and punching your brother, and after
you cried in your bedroom for hours.
And say that the lodger
was really your father, no, *say*.

Birds in the Blue Night

Each time, the live tangle of birds,
blue in the blue night, circling at the high window
I did not leave open, surely.

Not birds I know, dank-feathered, inky-eyed,
spinning in a ring until one breaks free, flies in.
And already I am out of bed

and on the path to my father's room,
the whole house sleeping but for him, his old face
stunned in the white light webbed on the wall

and I say *Dad, the bird in my room.*
Each time he rises, my shadow on the carpet
follows where he passes,

watches in the doorway as he softly coos
and scoops the bird into his palms, strange trophy
thrown out into the night again.

Memorial

A child you've never met takes your photograph to school.
The others pin you to the classroom wall
beside Jamaica stitched in green and turquoise felt.
Sugar paper women dance calypso under
cardboard palm trees and the photocopied gaze
of solemn Arawaks, Caribs, Maroons.

At home, she hides her drawings down behind the bed,
writes a letter: *Uncle Ralph was born in Yallahs Bay*
a long long time ago. I love him and I miss him.
She's shaded you in brown crayon, lying flat and dead
below a field of scribbled grass and coloured birds,
a yellow-pencil orb, the old Jamaica sun.

Those Long Car Silences

All those long car silences, the miles and miles
you drove me through this city, strange signs
lit up in neon, *Lucky House, The Taj Mahal, Halal.*

I kept my voice held back for nothing
but to punish you. I see us from the outside now,
our tail-lights disappearing in the rain

around the corner, down the street, through the shadow
of a railway bridge. You wanted me to get us lost,
a game you thought I'd like. You had to follow

my instructions *turn right, turn left.* We crossed
the river, past a broken clock tower, a monolithic factory
then rows and rows of battered council blocks,

their windows, dominoes of light. I strained to see
the figures moving through the glass in silhouette,
the orange glint of cigarettes on balconies.

Of course you always knew your way, the city's orbit
mapped by dim-lit poker clubs where you had played
from Ladbroke Grove to Bow to Forest Gate

and I would never say more than I had to say.
Now you come to me in dreams, the details varied
but the same. It's late, I'm in a stranger's hallway,

always leaving, stepping out into the road,
the rain, the hollow slam behind me of a door
and there you are, waiting in the battered Ford,

its engine running soft below the yellow blur
of streetlamp. Wordlessly, I climb into the car.

A Man Can Cook

You at the stove, the air spiced up with ginger,
nutmeg, clove. I know you won't turn round
but I can stand here can't I, watch the fire
flaring blue below your pans, your hands
cajoling dumpling, knifing up red snapper,
crushing star anise? You can't turn round,
too busy with your strange colonial mixtures,
mango roly poly, cocoa bread.
My aunty said 'Now *there's* a man can *cook!*'
I should have let you teach me, long before
you couldn't eat, before they sliced a moon
of flesh away from you. Now you're blurred
by steam. These smells will linger in my hair.
I leave you here then, humming as you stir.

Grief Was the Flash Bloke

with bleached teeth and a tan. He stood at the grave
in suede coat, gold chain, head low. Back at the wake
mourners stood in clusters, drank and chain-smoked,
sighed the same pale words of woe and grief.
He grabbed you at the door and pressed a packet
in your hand. You wondered where you'd met
before, or why he'd buy you flights to Spain
or write directions to a whitewashed villa
in the hills, but were glad he had:
two weeks of hot clean sun almost made you forget.
Years later, he's sat at the bar of your local: frailer,
shabby, pale, and he keeps saying *your dad,*
your dad, as his fingers twist his cigarette.

The Day

The sun does arise, and make happy the skies
WILLIAM BLAKE

We took the wild path from *The Smugglers' Arms*
across the chalk man's limbs, down the hill
towards the sea. We were small bright things
crouched by sandcastles and moats. We danced
across the dunes. There was one black man
on the beach and he buried me deep in the cold wet sand.

The day was made from spades and buckets, sand
and seagulls, salted air and sunburnt arms,
from waves that tugged the shore where the black man
stood in rolled up jeans, the scraggy hills
around the beach, the breakers that we danced
between. We only knew this way of things.

We plucked the shells and pebbles, shiny things,
our keepsakes. We wrote our names into the sand
and swam the tide to where a red buoy danced
on the wide blue water. We called and raised our arms
but the waves were rough, as high as hills.
We couldn't catch the eye of the black man

watching on the pier. Behind, the chalk man
loomed. We didn't understand these things.
The black man said the Saxons etched the hill,
their effigy, more fixed than names in sand
like ours. I lay back in the black man's arms
as he talked and watched the others dance,

red children at the shore, a long slow dance
for the day's end. In the sand, the black man
wrote his name. I lay on spindly arms
of seaweed. Then we gathered up our things –
goodbye, goodbye – and ran across the sand
clambering up, away, across the hill.

We turned back once to look from the top of the hill.
His name had disappeared and seaweed danced
in silhouette across the level sand.
The sun had set and down the beach the black man,
a tiny figure, walked on to other things
as we did, on the wild path, arm in arm,

trailing sand across the darkening hill.
Then slowly past *The Smugglers' Arms* we danced –
the beach, the sea, the black man, lost, forgotten things.